PEOPLE IN THE NEWS

Michelle Obama

First Lady, Author, and Activist

By Kristen Rajczak Nelson

Portions of this book originally appeared in
Michelle Obama by Michael V. Uschan.

LUCENT
PRESS

Published in 2020 by
Lucent Press, an Imprint of Greenhaven Publishing, LLC
353 3rd Avenue
Suite 255
New York, NY 10010

Designer: Deanna Paternostro
Editor: Kristen Rajczak Nelson

Library of Congress Cataloging-in-Publication Data

Names: Rajczak Nelson, Kristen, author.
Title: Michelle Obama : first lady, author, and activist / Kristen Rajczak
   Nelson.
Description: New York : Lucent Press, 2020. | Series: People in the news |
   Includes bibliographical references and index.
Identifiers: LCCN 2018059350 (print) | LCCN 2018060795 (ebook) | ISBN
   9781534567764 (eBook) | ISBN 9781534567757 (pbk. book) | ISBN
   9781534567085 (library bound book)
Subjects: LCSH: Obama, Michelle, 1964– | Obama, Michelle, 1964– |
Presidents' spouses—United States—Biography. | African American lawyers—
Biography.
   | Political activists—Biography.
Classification: LCC E909.O24 (ebook) | LCC E909.O24 R35 2020 (print) | DDC
   973.932092—dc23
LC record available at https://lccn.loc.gov/2018059350

Printed in the United States of America

CPSIA compliance information: Batch #BS19KL: For further information contact Greenhaven Publishing LLC, New York,
New York, at 1-844-317-7404.

Please visit our website, www.greenhavenpublishing.com. For a free color
catalog of all our high-quality books, call toll free 1-844-317-7404 or fax
1-844-317-7405.

Contents

Foreword

We live in a world where the latest news is always available and where it seems we have unlimited access to the lives of the people in the news. Entire television networks are devoted to news about politics, sports, and entertainment. Social media has allowed people to have an unprecedented level of interaction with celebrities. We have more information at our fingertips than ever before. However, how much do we really know about the people we see on television news programs, social media feeds, and magazine covers?

Despite the constant stream of news, the full stories behind the lives of some of the world's most newsworthy men and women are often unknown. Who was Gal Gadot before she became Wonder Woman? What does LeBron James do when he is not playing basketball? What inspires Lin-Manuel Miranda?

This series aims to answer questions like these about some of the biggest names in pop culture, sports, politics, and technology. While the subjects of this series come from all walks of life and areas of expertise, they share a common magnetism that has made them all captivating figures in the public eye. They have shaped the world in some unique way, and—in many cases—they are poised to continue to shape the world for many years to come.

These biographies are not just a collection of basic facts. They tell compelling stories that show how each figure grew to become a powerful public personality. Each book aims to paint a complete, realistic picture of its subject—from the challenges they overcame to the controversies they caused. In doing so, each book reinforces the idea that even the most famous faces on the news are real people who are much more complex than we are often shown in brief video clips or sound bites. Readers are also reminded that there is even more to a person than what they present to the world through social media posts, press releases, and interviews. The whole story of a person's life can only be discovered by digging beneath the surface of their public persona, and that is what this series allows readers to do.

The books in this series are filled with enlightening quotes from speeches and interviews given by the subjects, as well as quotes and anecdotes from those who know their story best: family, friends, coaches, and colleagues. All quotes are noted to provide guidance for further research. Detailed lists of additional resources are also included, as are timelines, indexes, and unique photographs. These text features come together to enhance the reading experience and encourage readers to dive deeper into the stories of these influential men and women.

Fame can be fleeting, but the subjects featured in this series have real staying power. They have fundamentally impacted their respective fields and have achieved great success through hard work and true talent. They are men and women defined by their accomplishments, and they are often seen as role models for the next generation. They have left their mark on the world in a major way, and their stories are meant to inspire readers to leave their mark, too.

A Groundbreaking Role Model

On February 12, 2018, the official portraits of Barack and Michelle Obama were unveiled at the Smithsonian National Portrait Gallery. They immediately made history, becoming the first presidential portraits that had been commissioned to black artists. Art critics across the country spent thousands of words on their color and composition, and what they meant to the future of American art. Thousands of visitors ambled through the gallery to take in the final sign the Obama years in the White House were over. They tweeted and emailed their thoughts about the paintings all over the world.

However, it was the story of one little black girl that truly captured the meaning of what the portrait of the first black First Lady would mean going forward. In February 2018, Parker Curry, then two years old, visited the National Portrait Gallery with her mother and younger sister. She knew who Michelle was because she had seen her dance on *The Ellen DeGeneres Show*.

As Parker approached the painting, she was "captivated," her mother, Jessica Curry, remembered later. "I called her name repeatedly, trying to get her to turn around so I could take a photo of her looking at the camera ... but she was motionless, completely absorbed in the grandeur of the image."[1] Parker's amazement was caught in a photo by a minister from North Carolina. He posted it online.

Soon, the image of a tiny black girl standing in front of the huge portrait of Michelle Obama had gone viral. One commenter wrote, "This is what America is all about. This young girl can now dream about being someone like Michelle Obama."[2] Another chimed in: "She'll grow up with the belief that *she* could be President. That black women are equally as fabulous and capable as any other American."[3]

The responses to the photo of Parker echoed what Michelle Obama had said herself when her portrait was unveiled not long before: "I'm also thinking about all the young people—particularly girls and girls of color—who in years ahead will come to this place and they will look up and they will see an image of someone who looks like them hanging on the wall of this great American institution."[4]

Once Michelle learned about Parker and her belief that the First Lady was "a queen,"[5] she invited Parker to her office to meet, and they danced to Taylor Swift's "Shake It Off." This perfectly embodied the spirit Michelle put into her role as First Lady: a care for and genuine connection with the American people, particularly young people. Michelle welcomed people of all ages, family backgrounds, and economic circumstances into the best-known house in the United States. She mentored teenage girls and planted a prodigious garden. She advocated for veterans and supported artists. And beyond these initiatives, Michelle quietly, boldly represented something greater—inclusion.

However wide-reaching her platform became, Michelle never stopped seeing herself as the approval-seeking achiever from the South Side of Chicago, Illinois. She spent the early years of her career and marriage questioning her own path in life, and then the path chosen by her husband. She reluctantly entered the world of politics with reservations about losing herself, damaging her daughters' childhood, and opening her private world to this very public arena. Yet, the importance of what she believed her husband could do on the national stage—and by extension, what

Michelle's official portrait was painted by Amy Sherald, the first black woman artist to be commissioned to paint a First Lady.

she could do—eventually overrode these worries. She realized the eyes of the country—and history—were on her as the first black First Lady. She decided, as she said in her final remarks as First Lady in 2017, to "lead by example with hope; never fear."[6]

Chapter **One**

From the South Side to the Ivy League

Long before Michelle Obama set foot in the best-known house in the United States, she lived with her family in a rented apartment in the South Shore neighborhood on the South Side of Chicago, Illinois. She was a smart, determined girl from a young age, eager to keep up with her older brother and encouraged by the love and belief of her parents. Through the obstacles of her young life, Michelle became strong and willing to do the work needed to get what she wanted. Her early determination foreshadowed the inspiring woman she would become.

At Home with the Robinsons

Michelle LaVaughn Robinson was born in Chicago on January 17, 1964. Her parents were Fraser Robinson III, a city water plant employee, and Marian Shields Robinson, a stay-at-home mom. She had an older brother, Craig. Michelle said her parents created a tight-knit, loving family atmosphere that made her feel protected: "[My dad] and my mom poured everything they had into me and Craig. It was the greatest gift a child could receive, never doubting for a single minute that you were loved and cherished and have a place in this world."[7]

The family rented the upper floor of a small, two-story home in Chicago's South Shore area from a great-aunt, a school teacher who lived on the first floor and taught piano. They had so little space that Fraser built a partition in the living room so Michelle and Craig could have their own bedrooms.

Michelle and Craig remained close throughout the time Michelle was First Lady of the United States.

Michelle Obama's
Ties to Black History

Jim Robinson, Michelle's great-great-grandfather, was born a slave in 1850 in Georgetown, South Carolina. In the early 1930s, Fraser Robinson Jr., Michelle's grandfather, moved to Chicago, Illinois. He was one of millions of black Americans who moved to northern states to escape racism in the South during the first half of the 20th century. Racism was less overt in northern states, but even into the 1960s, African Americans in Chicago went to segregated schools, lived in segregated communities, and faced job discrimination.

The year Michelle was born, the Civil Rights Act of 1964 passed. This landmark law made it illegal to discriminate against someone based on the color of their skin or their sex, religion, race, or national origin. No longer could public places or schools be segregated, and according to the law, everyone had the right to vote. While the law did not immediately end discrimination, it provided a legal basis for black Americans to fight back against it. In the summer of 1966, two years after Michelle was born, civil rights leader Martin Luther King Jr. protested segregated housing and education in Chicago. Violence erupted during marches he led into white areas. This was the backdrop of Michelle's early childhood: a United States in which racism was still alive and well, even beyond the South.

Michelle idolized her dad. In addition to being a loving father, Fraser was also a hero to her because he continued working despite living with multiple sclerosis (MS), a disease in which the body slowly attacks the nervous system, eventually causing the brain to cease proper communication with the rest of the body, particularly harming muscle control. Michelle said,

> My dad was our rock. And although he was diagnosed with multiple sclerosis in his early 30s, he was our provider. He was our champion, our hero. [If] he was in pain, he never let on. He never stopped smiling and laughing, even while struggling to button his shirt, even while using two canes to get himself across the room to give my mom a kiss. He just woke up a little earlier and he worked a little harder.[8]

Michelle as a Child

When Michelle was little, she loved riding her bike. She had an Easy Bake Oven, played with her dollhouse, and loved Barbie dolls. According to Marian Robinson, Michelle was an intelligent, independent little girl: "I always say Michelle raised herself from about nine years old. She had her head on straight very early."[9] Michelle has said this was a product of her parents child-rearing philosophy: "My parents talked to us like we were adults. They didn't lecture, but rather indulged every question we asked, no matter how juvenile. They never hurried a discussion for the sake of convenience."[10]

The Robinsons lived a quiet, family-oriented life. They ate their meals together and often played board games, such as Chinese checkers and Monopoly. Michelle and Craig learned to play the piano from a young age from their great-aunt downstairs. They also spent a lot of time visiting family members who lived around the Chicago area. Michelle was especially close to Southside, her maternal grandfather, who kept a dog named Rex for her and Craig and played jazz albums whenever the family visited.

At School

Both of Michelle's parents believed a good education would

Michelle has always relied on her mother (center) for good advice and support.

help their children be successful even though neither parent had attended college. However, as some of the wealthier and white families moved out of their neighborhood to the suburbs, their neighborhood schools began to decline. In second grade, Michelle found herself in a class with a teacher who did not seem to care—and Michelle did, deeply. She spoke to her mother, who then went to the head of the school. After a few tests, Michelle and some other bright students in the class were moved up to third grade. Michelle later called it "a small but life-changing move."[11]

Learning About the
Political Process

Michelle's dad, Fraser Robinson III, was a Democratic Party precinct captain who helped register voters. As a child, Michelle was exposed to his work within the Democratic Party and remembered her observations of the political process at its lowest levels:

Some of my earliest memories are of tagging along with him as we'd walk door to door and help folks register to vote. We'd sit in neighbors' kitchens for hours and listen to their opinions, their concerns, and the dreams they had for their children. And before we left those kitchens, my father would make sure that everyone could get to the voting booth on Election Day—because he knew that a single vote could help make their dreams a reality.[1]

Her father's position also left Michelle with a negative opinion of politics in general. Her father was pressured to take on his position with the Democratic Party in Chicago in order to rise in his job. While they knew the value of parts of being a precinct captain, the general corruption in Chicago politics remained distasteful to him and, later, Michelle.

1. Quoted in David Colbert, *Michelle Obama: An American Story*. New York, NY: Houghton Mifflin Harcourt, 2009, pp. 10–11.

Michelle continued to be one of the brightest students in her class, but she had to work hard at it. Craig, on the other hand, was a gifted student who did not have to study all night to do well in school. Michelle worked so hard that she even impressed Craig, who said, "I'd come home from basketball practice, and she'd be working. I'd sit down on the couch and watch TV; she'd keep working. When I turned off the TV, she'd still be working."[12] Socializing did not come as easily to Michelle as it did to Craig either. Craig mixed easily with all the kids in the changing landscape of the Robinsons' neighborhood. Michelle spent more time crafting elaborate stories and adventures for her Barbies than making friends around her neighborhood for much of her early childhood.

School was Michelle's priority. By the time Michelle was in sixth grade, she was in the gifted class at school. She studied French for three years and took advanced biology classes.

Although a neighborhood public high school was only a block away from the Robinson home, Michelle, like her brother, chose to attend a more academically difficult school. Craig had enrolled in Mount Carmel, a private boys' school with tough academic standards and an outstanding sports program. The latter was important for Craig, a talented 6-foot, 5-inch (1.96 m) basketball player, who would become good enough to win an athletic scholarship to college. Michelle decided to attend Whitney M. Young, Chicago's first magnet high school. Michelle began high school in 1977, two years after Whitney M. Young opened.

Whitney M. Young had more black students than white students. Among the students were the children of the city's most influential African Americans, including Santita Jackson, the daughter of Baptist minister and civil rights activist Jesse Jackson. Going to Whitney M. Young separated Michelle not only geographically from her old neighborhood but also culturally, because many of her fellow students' families were better off financially than hers was. However, Michelle's intelligence and commitment to hard work helped her excel again academically. She made the honor roll all four years and became a member of the National Honor Society. In her senior year, Michelle was elected student council treasurer. By the end of her time there, she had gained confidence in herself—enough to follow her brother to the Ivy League.

Michelle chose Whitney M. Young even though it could take more than an hour each way for her to get there. She visited the school and spoke to students there in 2018.

Princeton

If it had not been for her brother, Michelle Obama might never have attended Princeton University in Princeton, New Jersey. Princeton is an Ivy League school, or one of a small group of expensive private universities in the northeast United States whose students are historically from rich, white families. However, after Craig Robinson received an athletic scholarship to Princeton, Michelle decided to go there too. She said,

Politics Up Close

In high school, Michelle became close friends with Santita Jackson, the daughter of Jesse Jackson—a famous civil rights activist and politician. At the time, Reverend Jackson was just a few years away from becoming the first major black presidential candidate. Michelle saw his children attend campaign events and protests: "They'd stood on stages in front of big crowds and were learning to absorb the anxiety and controversy that came with having a father, maybe especially a black father, in public life."[1]

Michelle and Santita ended up on TV marching with Jesse Jackson's supporters during a parade. It was an important event for black leaders in Chicago, but Michelle did not care for the attention she felt as part of it:

What I knew was that I personally didn't love the feeling of being out there, thrust under a baking sun amid balloons and bullhorns, amid trombones and throngs of cheering people. The fanfare was fun and even intoxicating, but there was something about it, and about politics in general, that made me queasy.[2]

These lessons, like those she learned from her father's work with the Illinois Democratic Party, would stay with her, informing her opinions on politics and politicians for years to come.

1. Michelle Obama, *Becoming*. New York, NY: Crown Publishing Group, 2018, p. 63.

2. Obama, *Becoming*, p. 64.

That was really my first exposure to the possibility of the Ivy League. It wasn't that I couldn't get in, or I couldn't thrive, or I couldn't survive. I didn't know to [even] want that. That wasn't the vision that I could see for myself because I couldn't see anybody around me doing that.[13]

When Michelle decided on Princeton, she went to a guidance counselor at Whitney M. Young for help in filling out Princeton's application. The counselor told Michelle she might not be the right kind of student for Princeton. Michelle has said that she left the office angry: "She was telling me to lower my sights, which was the absolute reverse of every last thing my parents had ever told me."[14]

The College Experience

At Whitney M. Young, the black students outnumbered the white students. However, in 1981, on Princeton's campus, Michelle would find herself in the minority. Michelle was one of only 94 African Americans out of the school's 1,141 freshmen students. There were also very few black teachers at Princeton. Men outnumbered the women on campus as well. Michelle was only 17 when she started at Princeton and thrown into a social situation unlike anything she had experienced before: "I'd never stood out in a crowd or a classroom because of the color of my skin. It was jarring and uncomfortable, at least at first, like being dropped into a strange new terrarium, a habitat that hadn't been built for me."[15]

The small group of black students felt alienated from the white students. The unease some whites felt toward blacks included Michelle's first roommate—or at least her roommate's family. When Michelle arrived on campus in September 1981, she shared a dormitory room with Catherine Donnelly, who was from Louisiana. When Donnelly told her family she had a black roommate, her mother was so upset that she demanded school officials move her daughter to another room and even threatened to remove her from Princeton. Donnelly moved to another room at the end of the first semester. Michelle never knew what Donnelly's family had done until 2008, when a newspaper reporter contacted her after talking to the Donnelly family. Michelle said she was never close with Donnelly, but that maybe an unease with a black woman was the reason.

There was an economic as well as a racial barrier between students because most of the white students were from wealthy families and had much more money than Michelle and other black students. Michelle's working-class parents could not afford her tuition, much less her expenses. In order to

Although Princeton was founded in 1746, it did not allow women to enroll as undergraduates until 1969. Princeton was also segregated for much of its existence.

attend Princeton, Michelle had to obtain financial aid from the school and take out student loans. She had a work-study job assisting the director at the Third World Center, a place on campus specifically established to help students of color at Princeton.

Embracing Race

Michelle and other minority students at Princeton, including black, Hispanic, Jewish, and Asian students, tended to hang out together at the Third World Center. Michelle admits that the center became a safe haven for black students like herself. They had big meals together and dance parties. It was here that she became close friends with Suzanne Alele, a Nigerian woman raised in Jamaica. Suzanne, described by Michelle as a free spirit who "based most of her decisions … on how fun it was likely to be,"[16] would become a great force in Michelle's life at Princeton and beyond.

There was not a lot of time for having fun, however, because Michelle was so busy studying and working. She began coordinating an after-school day care center at the Third World Center. She also worked during the summer to earn money for books and tuition, instead of taking the unpaid internships other students might use to build their resumes.

Michelle's experiences as a black woman at Princeton affected her so deeply that she decided to write about race in the senior thesis that was a requirement for graduation. It was titled "Princeton-Educated Blacks and the Black Community." In it, Michelle wrote that Princeton gave blacks a quality education that helped them achieve success in their chosen fields. She also noted, though, that blacks often felt uncomfortable socially at Princeton and claimed those uneasy feelings were because the school seemed to care more about white students. She also surveyed black graduates, finding that other black Princeton graduates also cared as she did for those in black communities who did not have the chance at an Ivy League education and network. This discovery bolstered her desire to make a difference for her community.

By her final year, Michelle had proven to herself and those around her that she belonged and could compete with the best and brightest around her. She later expressed this was done at a cost: "Beneath my laid-back college-kid demeanor, I lived like a half-closeted CEO, quietly but unswervingly focused on achievement, bent on checking every box. My to-do list lived in my head and went with me everywhere."[17] To her, the right thing to do as an articulate, critical thinker was to head to law school—and not just any law school: Harvard Law School. Looking back, Michelle said that she was driven by the approval of others, and this next step was an impressive one. She would excel, but it was a path she would come to question.

Chapter **Two**

Harvard, Law, and Love

As Michelle embarked on law school and then started her career, she silently questioned if her choices thus far had been the right ones. She became known at Harvard Law School as a well-spoken, determined woman who was not afraid to confront a difficult question. Whatever path she chose following graduation, it was clear she would succeed—and she did. Michelle had an impressive job and salary with an office and assistant—perfect for a new lawyer attempting to pay off student loans taken out for two Ivy League schools. However, she felt a desire to give back to the black community around her and engage with those who did not have the privileges she now did.

When a young black lawyer named Barack Obama came into her life, Michelle was still grappling with these issues. When it turned out that Barack also had a deeply held commitment to service within the black community, Michelle eventually felt encouraged to follow her own path—and she began to want that path to be the same one Barack would walk.

Harvard Law School

Charles J. Ogletree, Michelle's adviser at Harvard, said by the time Michelle began attending Harvard in 1985, she had figured out what it meant to be an African American woman in a world dominated by whites. According to Ogletree, "Princeton was a real crossroads of identity for Michelle … by the time she got to Harvard she had answered the question. She could be both brilliant and black."[18] Her new connection to her racial identity may have played a role in Michelle's reasons to become a lawyer, too. As she wrote in her Princeton senior thesis on race,

> *There was no doubt in my mind that as a member of the Black community I was somehow obligated to this community and would utilize all of my present and future resources to benefit this community first and foremost. This realization has presently, made my goals to actively utilize my resources to benefit the Black community more desirable.*[19]

Michelle experienced this firsthand while working at the Harvard Legal Aid Bureau. Run entirely by law students, the bureau provides legal assistance in civil cases to people who cannot afford lawyers. Law students usually work 20 hours a week for the bureau, a huge commitment considering how hard their studies are. Michelle has called her time working there the happiest of her days as a Harvard Law student.

Michelle belonged to several African American organizations at Harvard, including the *Harvard BlackLetter Law Journal*, whose members wrote about legal issues, and the Black Law Student Association, which was mainly a social club for African American students on the nearly all-white campus. While Michelle was at Harvard, she wrote an essay titled "Minority and Women Law Professors: A Comparison of Teaching Styles," which spoke of the need for more women and minorities as professors. She argued that both people of color and women could reach students in different ways more traditional

Speaking Her Mind

Harvard Law School's reputation as the nation's finest law school is based on its high academic standards. Michelle's fellow students and her professors were impressed with her academic abilities as a student. One professor, David Wilkins, said she was a thinker and often spoke her mind, but also listened well. He recalled her conviction coming through in class: "She was always the person who was asking the question, 'What does this have to do with providing real access and real justice for real people? Is that fair? Is this right?' She was always very clear on those questions."[1]

1. Quoted in Peter Slevin, *Michelle Obama: A Life*. New York, NY: Alfred A. Knopf, 2015, p. 108.

faculty members could not. Her essay was part of a bigger movement among the black students at Harvard. Months later, some members of the Black Law Student Association staged a sit-in in support of a document of demands that included adding a black female law professor immediately to the faculty.

Michelle earned her law degree from Harvard Law School in 1988. Her professor David Wilkins said he spoke to Michelle and her family at the gradation:

Harvard Law School is a hard place. It's a hard place for anybody, but it's a particularly hard place for black students and more for black women students. Michelle not only did well in this place, but she did something quite unique: She tried to change it. I don't know what your daughter's going to do, but I promise you, what she decides to do, she's going to be somebody special.[20]

Michelle left Harvard and Princeton with a great education—but a lot of student loan debt. Taking a lucrative job seemed like a good way to pay it off.

Michelle returned home to Chicago to begin her career as a lawyer with Sidley & Austin, a firm known today as Sidley Austin LLP.

Part of the Firm

Like other firms, Sidley & Austin hired law students each summer. It did that to give the students experience and to assess their talent to see if they would be worth hiring when they graduated. Michelle had worked there during the summer of 1987. The firm liked her so much that it hired her a year later and assigned her to the firm's division that dealt with marketing and copyright issues. The division's clients included companies that sold products ranging from automobiles to beer, as well as some that produced various forms of entertainment, including television shows. One of Michelle's first important projects was to work on legal questions regarding the marketing of *Barney*, a new children's show at the time that became an instant hit.

Michelle was working as a lawyer in one of Chicago's most noted legal firms. From the start, though, it did not feel right to Michelle. She did not spend much time talking to clients, instead spending hours alone with documents for the cases she was assigned. She and the other junior associates worked 70 hours a week, which left little time for forming friendships. Michelle felt somewhat isolated. In order to save money to make her large student loan payments each month, Michelle was living above her parents in the same apartment she grew up in on the South Side. They did not charge her rent, and she was able to hug her mom and dad every day. That alone helped her get through her days on a high floor of a building she could only dream about working in when she took the bus to high school years before.

Enter: Barack Obama

When Michelle was at at Sidley & Austin, there were only about five full-time black attorneys. In 1989, senior partners in the firm asked her to be the adviser for Barack Obama, a first-year law student who had been hired for the summer. The partners chose Michelle because they respected her and because Barack was attending Harvard Law School, her alma mater.

Michelle knew a little about Barack before she met him. Because Sidley & Austin did not usually hire first-year law students, Michelle realized Barack must have been highly intelligent to have been hired. Some of the women in the office had also told her that Barack was handsome and had a great personality, but Michelle's future husband failed to impress her when they had lunch to get to know each other. She said,

> He sounded too good to be true. I had dated a lot of brothers who had this kind of [smart and charismatic] reputation going in, so I figured he was one of these smooth brothers who could talk straight and impress people. So we had lunch, and he had this bad sports jacket and a cigarette dangling from his mouth, and I thought "Oh, here you go. Here's this good-looking, smooth-talking guy. I've been down this road before."[21]

As his adviser, Michelle helped Barack get used to working in the large law firm. She educated him about various office procedures, helped him acclimate socially, and was available to answer questions he had. Earlier that year, Michelle had told her mother that she was going to concentrate on her career and had no time for dating. While Barack started asking her to go out as more than just friends, Michelle tried to fix him up with her friends instead. However, after spending time with Barack that summer, she began to change her mind, even though she worried how it would be perceived in her workplace.

Finally, after a company social event, Michelle began to acknowledge her feelings for Barack. She remembers looking at him and thinking, "He's a good person."[22] He recalls of that afternoon: "After a firm picnic, she drove me back to my apartment and I offered to buy her an ice cream at the Baskin-Robbins store across the street. We sat on the curb

Barack Hussein Obama II was born on August 4, 1961, in Honolulu, Hawaii. He was named after his father, Barack Obama Sr., a Kenyan native. His mother, Ann Dunham, was white and had been born in Wichita, Kansas.

and ate our ice creams in the sticky afternoon heat. [When we finished eating] I asked if I could kiss her. It tasted of chocolate."[23]

Soon after the ice cream date, they went out in public as a couple for the first time to see *Do the Right Thing*, a movie by director Spike Lee. Their romance got serious quickly as they talked about everything under the sun—the best Stevie Wonder albums, movies, and of course, the state of the world around them.

As they got to know each other better, Michelle discovered that Barack had grown up very differently from her stable household of four on the South Side. Most of his time growing up had been spent in Hawaii and Indonesia. At times, she

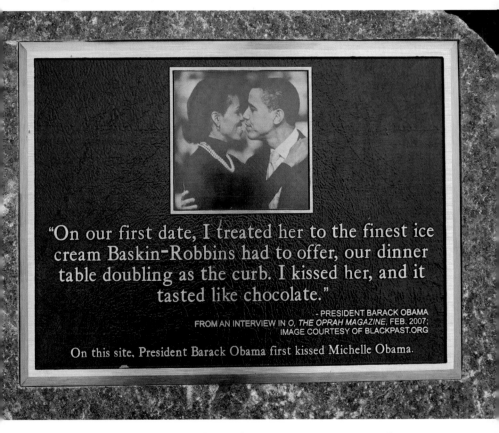

"On our first date, I treated her to the finest ice cream Baskin-Robbins had to offer, our dinner table doubling as the curb. I kissed her, and it tasted like chocolate."

- PRESIDENT BARACK OBAMA
FROM AN INTERVIEW IN *O, THE OPRAH MAGAZINE*, FEB. 2007;
IMAGE COURTESY OF BLACKPAST.ORG

On this site, President Barack Obama first kissed Michelle Obama.

This plaque in Hyde Park in Chicago commemorates the Obamas' first kiss.

questioned whether she had enough in common with someone with such a different background from herself. However, when she met his mother, half-sister Maya, and the grandparents who helped raise him in Hawaii, her view changed: "They were a modest, middle-class family, in many ways not at all unlike my own. There was something comforting in this, for both me and Barack. As different as we were, we fit together in an interesting way."[24]

Falling in Love

Michelle was still unsure about getting serious with Barack as they continued to spend more time together that summer. She learned he also deeply cared about bettering the community and had worked in Chicago before law school helping underserved neighborhoods organize and create jobs. She wrote in her memoir that realizing his desires to make the world a better place forced her to confront the questioning she felt about her own career. She likened her time as a lawyer to a tightly folded piece of origami:

> I was proud of how it looked. But it was delicate. If one corner came untucked, I might discover that I was restless. If another popped loose, it might reveal I was uncertain about the professional path I'd so deliberately put myself on … He [Barack] was like a wind that threatened to unsettle everything.[25]

Later that summer, Barack took her to a community meeting in a poor black area. He had worked there in his previous community organizing job and was returning to talk to people he knew. The meeting was in a church basement. As Barack spoke, Michelle was stunned at the eloquence and the power of the speech he delivered to the group of African Americans. He told them everyone had to commit themselves to fighting to make things better for not only themselves but also other people. Michelle said it was then that she opened her heart to the man she would marry. "What I saw in him on that day

In 2016, a movie about Michelle and Barack's first date was released. It was called *Southside With You*.

was authenticity and truth and principle. That's who I fell in love with, that man."[26] She saw that he believed in hope, and it was beyond the hope she had ever considered. She later wrote that his speech made her realize that "it was one thing to get yourself out of a stuck place … It was another thing entirely to try and get the place itself unstuck."[27]

Chapter **Three**

Big
Changes

So much changed in Michelle's life after meeting Barack—though her gain of him was sadly balanced by the loss of a good friend and her father. Reflective of what her life's work would be, Michelle made a career change away from her lucrative job at the law firm. Barack's career path soon began to become clearer, too, though not in a way Michelle readily accepted. From the very start, Michelle was wary of the effect political life would have on her, Barack, and their eventual family. Still, she began to support his efforts all the while succeeding in her own career.

Relationship Growth and Change

When Michelle began to get serious about Barack, she took him home to meet her parents to see what they thought of him. She also had her brother play basketball with Barack because Craig and their father believed that people reveal their true character in athletic competition. Barack passed the test by proving he was an unselfish player and an on-court leader. "He was aggressive without being a jerk, and I was able to report back to my sister that this guy is first-rate,"[28] Craig Robinson said. His seal of approval helped Barack pass an important test to winning Michelle's affection.

After Barack returned to Harvard that fall, he and Michelle maintained a long-distance relationship. They grew closer over the next two years, talking on the phone as much as they could despite their busy schedules—and hers did remain full.

In addition to her work as a lawyer, Michelle was one of the Sidley & Austin team that recruited new summer associates and lawyers. She made it her mission in this role to bring in more women and more people of color. She encouraged the other recruiters to look beyond the traditional law schools—including Harvard, Yale, and the University of Chicago—to find more diverse candidates. Nonetheless, she still found herself at Harvard for recruiting trips while Barack was there, giving the young couple much needed face-to-face time together.

Barack planned to move back to Chicago after he graduated from Harvard. Until then, Michelle was there in the second-floor apartment above her parents, reading more because of Barack's influence and trying to stay in touch with her friends, including Suzanne Alele and Santita Jackson, as they moved around the country. Suzanne's life was so different from Michelle's structured days at Sidley & Austin. Later, Michelle expressed that she often disagreed with how Suzanne was living her life at the time. So when Suzanne was diagnosed with cancer, Michelle began to examine Suzanne's free-spirited approach to life—and continue to question her own. Michelle put off visiting her friend in disbelief that her condition was serious. When another friend told Michelle to visit if she wanted to see Suzanne again, Michelle went. She held Suzanne's hand as she died at age 26 in June 1990.

Barack's ambition and drive contributed to Michelle's examination of her career and life goals, too. When he stayed with her in Chicago the summer of 1990 following Suzanne's death, Michelle was poised for introspection: "In the presence of his certainty, his notion that he could make some sort of difference in the world, I couldn't help but feel a little bit lost by

Barack read a lot and thought deeply about many things. He influenced Michelle to do more of the same.

comparison. His sense of purpose seemed like an unwitting challenge to my own."[29] As the year wore on, Michelle would turn this idea over in her mind further.

Life-Changing Loss

In addition to questioning her path in life, Michelle saw up close how her father's health was declining as his MS became more serious. However, he refused to go to the doctor. Eventually, he was not able to walk at all, and he was taken to the hospital by ambulance. Michelle, her mother, and her brother took turns visiting him—but it became clear medical help had come too late. Fraser Robinson III died on March 6, 1991, from a heart attack. Michelle had been with him as he had fallen asleep that night.

The deaths of her father and Suzanne magnified Michelle's discontent with her work. She wanted to be remembered for more than the legal briefs she was writing. The time had come to change her work life.

Career Shift

Michelle spent a few months meeting with people she admired or wanted to know more about around the city. This led her to meeting Valerie Jarrett, a black woman who had also gone to law school and left the law for different work. Valerie was working as the deputy chief of staff to the mayor of Chicago, Richard M. Daley. She offered Michelle a job in her office on the spot and even agreed to meet Barack to discuss the job with him and Michelle at dinner. In July 1991, Michelle left Sidley & Austin and began her work for the mayor. Barack, Michelle has written, was the number one person in her life encouraging her to embark on this new part of her career. He made her worry less about what was to come: "It was okay to make my leap into the unknown, because ... the unknown wasn't going to kill me."[30] Valerie was so impressed with Michelle's work that a year later, when she was named commissioner of the Chicago Department of Planning and

Committing to
Each Other

Though serious about Michelle, Barack was hesitant about getting married. By 1991, Michelle began to wonder if he would ever ask her to be his wife. Then one evening, Barack took Michelle to Gordon, an expensive Chicago restaurant. When the subject of getting married came up, Barack ticked off a list of reasons why they should not marry, including the fact that their love for each other was more important to their relationship than a marriage certificate. The discussion continued until dessert arrived—a plate bearing a small box. When Michelle opened the box and saw an engagement ring, Barack said, "That kind of shuts you up, doesn't it?"[1] He then asked Michelle to marry him.

1. Quoted in Liza Mundy, "When Michelle Met Barack," *Washington Post*, October 5, 2008.

Michelle married Barack Obama on October 3, 1992, at Trinity United Church of Christ in Chicago. Seventeen years later, they shared another first dance as president and First Lady of the United States.

Economic Development, she took Michelle with her as assistant commissioner.

Soon after their wedding in 1992, Barack was working for a nonprofit called Project VOTE!, which worked to register more minority voters and get them to the polls. Barack and Michelle were each engaging with the community around them in satisfying ways. However, in getting wrapped up in his work with Project VOTE!— which was very successful in the election that year—Barack had

missed a book deadline. He had been working on it while also serving on boards of nonprofits, promising to teach at the University of Chicago in the new semester, and starting full-time at a law firm. In order to finish it, he decided to take six weeks off and go to a quiet place in Indonesia with no distractions. Michelle understood his drive, but for the first time, life as Barack Obama's wife came into a new focus. It was a lonely six weeks for Michelle, still a new wife. It was a feeling she would come to know well.

Michelle knew Barack and Valerie would get along. They got along so well that Valerie would remain a good friend to each of them in the coming years.

Months later, after working nearly two years for the city of Chicago, Michelle changed jobs again. In 1993, she accepted the position of executive director of Public Allies, a nonprofit organization that encourages young people to get involved in public service. Michelle took the new position because she was excited about the challenges the new job presented: "It sounded risky and just out there. But for some reason it just spoke to me. This was the first time I said, 'this is what I say I care about. Right here.'"[31]

Michelle created the Chicago program from scratch, finding joy in discovering the right "allies" to train within the program. Under her leadership, Public Allies Chicago recruited young people from housing projects and youth centers as well as colleges and universities. Michelle liked that she had a chance to have an effect on the people she worked with. To her, the work she was doing finally had meaning.

After spending three years building perhaps the nation's strongest Public Allies program, Michelle was approached with yet another career opportunity. In the fall of 1996, she began working for the University of Chicago as an associate dean in community relations. Years earlier, she had met with a lawyer at the university named Art Sussman and told him that she had grown up near the University of Chicago but had never been inside it. Her role in community relations would tackle that reality, that those in the neighborhood surrounding the college did not engage with it, head on. She would go on to create a service program to bring students from the school into the Chicago community.

Political Aspirations

While Michelle was beginning to find professional fulfillment in positions that dealt directly with helping others, her husband, Barack, continued working for a small public interest firm as a civil rights attorney. He was also teaching constitutional law at the University of Chicago. When he was approached to consider running for an open seat in the Illinois State Senate in 1996, he saw it as a way to make a difference. Michelle did not want to stand in the way of her husband's dreams when he had been so encouraging of her career changes. Nonetheless, she did not trust politicians and doubted Barack could make a difference in public office. She said, "My view was, well, you can also impact a lot of people if you're the principal of a high school or a great teacher or a great dad. I wasn't a proponent of politics as a way you can make change."[32] Michelle was also worried about how much money her husband would have to spend to be elected and the extra time he would be away from home to campaign while still working as a law professor.

Michelle finally told him, "If that's what you really want to do, I think you'd be great at it. You're everything people say they want in their public officials."[33] She even admits to

Michelle's Reservations

Michelle never kept her worries about Barack becoming a politician to herself. Each time he ran for office, she voiced her opinion on it. Michelle wrote later that while her reasons for why he should not run changed a bit with each election, deep inside, she simply believed there were other ways for someone to have a positive impact on the world. Furthermore, she had seen how hard life was for both politicians and their families. She told Oprah Winfrey in 2018 that it was not a life she wanted for herself or Barack:

> I never wanted to be involved in politics. I had seen politics. I grew up in Chicago rough and tumble politics. And I knew Barack was a decent man. Smart ... but politics was ugly and nasty and I didn't know if my husband's temperament would mesh with that. And I didn't want to see him in that environment. But then on the flip side, you see the challenges the world is facing ... So I had to take off my wife hat and put on my citizen hat and say, "How can I stand in the way if I know that this man could do good?" The choice for him not to do it ... felt selfish and small. And I couldn't be the person that stopped it.[1]

She summed up her fears years later: "Quite honestly, I thought he'd get eaten alive."[2]

1. "Why Reluctant Michelle Obama Agreed to Let Barack Obama Run for President—Oprah's Book Club—OWN," YouTube video, 2:21, posted by OWN, November 12, 2018. www.youtube.com/watch?v=ICYb38sPXrs.

2. Michelle Obama, *Becoming*. New York, NY: Crown Publishing Group, 2018, p. 183.

In 1995, Barack published his first book, *Dreams from My Father*. It would not make much of an impact nationally until it was reissued years later.

enjoying being part of that first campaign, visiting their neighbors and collecting signatures while listening to their concerns. It reminded her of the times she went door to door with her father. In addition, some of what she liked about the campaign was that she was not needed very often and was free to continue her own work, which she was finding satisfying.

Chapter **Four**

More Than a Wife and Mother

While Barack headed into the fray of politics, Michelle stayed on her own career path. However, as their family grew, doubt crept in again that she was making the right choices:

> *I wanted to live with the hat-tossing, independent-career-woman zest of Mary Tyler Moore, and at the same time I gravitated toward the stabilizing, self-sacrificing, seemingly bland normalcy of being a wife and mother. I wanted to have a work life and a home life, but with some promise that one would never fully squelch the other.*[34]

As Barack found it increasingly hard to balance his time between Chicago and Springfield, where the legislature met, so too did Michelle find it hard to balance their growing family and furthering her career. She depended on her own adaptability and self-preservation during this time, qualities she would need as Barack's political aspirations trended toward Washington, D.C.

Raising a Family

Life changed for the Obamas when Barack won the election for Illinois State Senate. When the legislature was meeting, Barack had to spend part of each week in Springfield, the capital of Illinois. He now spent a lot of time away from home. The stories of Barack's work there did not convince Michelle that it was worth his time.

On July 4, 1998, Michelle and Barack had their first child, a daughter they named Malia Ann. Her birth came at an ideal time for Barack because the Illinois legislature was not in session. However, a few weeks later, when Barack had to return to Springfield, Michelle was left to care for Malia by herself for days at a time while also working full time. She switched to fewer hours on a flexible schedule at the University of Chicago, but her workload remained the same: "Part-time work was meant to give me more freedom, but mostly it left me feeling as if I were only half doing everything, that all the lines in my life had been blurred."[35]

Barack was soon elected to another term in the Illinois State Senate and began to contemplate a run for U.S. Congress as a representative of Illinois in 2000. Again, Michelle was not in favor of this move but consented. Barack lost in the primary.

On June 10, 2001, Michelle gave birth to Natasha, nicknamed Sasha. Barack continued to be away from home for long periods. This meant he was usually not around to eat supper with his family, read his kids a story, or do household chores to help Michelle. For several years, it was difficult for them to find a fair balance between work and family. However, Michelle also saw her husband's ambition and understood that she could not force him to take a regular job just to make him do more at home: "It's hard to look at

In addition to her work at the University of Chicago, Michelle served on the boards of nonprofit organizations, as did Barack. Their daughters and professional lives kept them very busy.

somebody with the talents and gifts of Barack and say, 'Go do something smaller than what you could do.'"[36]

When another opportunity came up, Michelle realized she needed to do something for herself. She was not happy with working part-time. Michelle wanted to make more money to get better help with child care and household responsibilities. Soon after Sasha was born, Michelle interviewed for a job as executive director of community affairs at the University of Chicago Medical Center. She felt she had to go into her interview with all her cards on the table: She was a working mother who needed the ability to manage her own schedule so that she could take care of her two small children. If flexibility like that would be available, Michelle believed she would truly be the best for the position.

Michelle was still on maternity leave when she went for the interview, and she had to bring three-month-old Sasha with her. Even in such unusual circumstances, Michelle got the job and looked forward to the goal of helping the South Side communities around her. However, having to take an infant to a job interview was only one of the problems she faced while trying to raise her daughters with Barack so often absent. Michelle knew something needed to change. She insisted she and Barack attend several counseling sessions in order to refocus their marriage, which she had begun to feel unhappy with. In these moments of intense communication, she realized her own agency in their living situation and her own happiness. She said,

> I spent a lot of time expecting my husband to fix things, but then I came to realize that he was there in the ways he could be. If he wasn't there, it didn't mean he wasn't a good father or didn't care. I saw it could be my mom or a great baby-sitter who helped. Once I was OK with that, my marriage got better.[37]

Michelle hired a housekeeper to cook, clean, and do laundry. She also began depending on her mother and a circle of good friends to babysit Malia and Sasha when necessary and help out in other ways. The freedom she gained allowed her to exercise and spend time relaxing with her children, two things that helped her feel more herself. Michelle set up a strict schedule for the girls, with an ironclad dinnertime and bedtime. No more would they be waiting around for Barack to come home from Springfield. While this made raising the girls a bit easier, Michelle saw her stance as even more meaningful than that:

> It went back to my wishes for them to grow up strong and centered and also unaccommodating to any form of old-school

patriarchy: I didn't want them ever to believe that life began when the man of the house arrived home. We didn't wait for Dad. It was his job now to catch up with us.[38]

The Senate Campaign

Barack's unsuccessful run for Congress and time in the state senate only made Michelle like politics less. Some of it was Barack's hectic schedule that did not seem to allow much time for his family. When the question of running for U.S. Senate in 2004 came up, her answer was not a resounding yes. Michelle "feared that the path he'd chosen for himself—and still seemed so clearly committed to pursuing—would end up steam-rolling our every need."[39] Michelle said she would agree to his running for the U.S. Senate with one caveat: If he lost, that was it. He would be out of politics and have to work in another job.

Michelle was enjoying her work at the hospital. She spread information about proper health care options to low-income neighborhoods through volunteer programs and student outreach, and even encouraged the hospital to support more minority-owned and women-owned businesses. However, now that Barack wanted to run for such a high office, she felt herself holding back. She wanted to keep Malia and Sasha's life as normal and stable as possible and sometimes that meant not going the extra mile with a young employee she was mentoring or passing off part of a project to someone else so she could go home and be Mom.

Barack's success in the Senate campaign was strengthened by Michelle, who made several effective campaign appearances for him. Her campaign stops helped build support for Barack, but when a reporter asked her what it was like to be the wife of a candidate, Michelle responded, "It's hard, and that's why Barack is such a grateful man."[40] Although Michelle said it in a joking manner, her remark was an admission that she did not find campaigning easy and was still worried about how the election would affect her family.

Michelle sacrificed more than her time campaigning for Barack. They took out a second mortgage to pay for the campaign.

Even though she began to accept Barack's path, Michelle still stood firmly in her knowledge that she had not chosen the life of a political spouse. To her, this understanding meant that she did not yet need to change her own life for her husband's career.

Nationally Known

Barack's candidacy also received a huge boost when the Democratic Party chose him to deliver the keynote address at its convention in Boston, Massachusetts. Because his televised speech on July 27, 2004, would be seen by tens of millions of people, Barack knew it was a chance to make himself nationally known. Michelle also knew how important the speech could be to his future, so to loosen him up before he went on stage, Michelle hugged Barack and said, "Just don't screw it up, buddy!"[41] In his speech, Barack recounted his unique heritage and said his success story could only have been possible in the United States. It was the highlight of the convention and made him an instant celebrity. Michelle knew then that this part of their lives was here to stay: "I quietly began to let go of the idea that there was any reversing his course, that he'd ever belong solely to me and the girls. I could almost hear it in the pulse of the applause."[42]

The speech carried Barack to victory in November to become a U.S. senator representing Illinois. When Barack was sworn in on January 3, 2005, Michelle, Malia, Sasha, and other family members watched from the Senate balcony. Barack had impressed so many people so deeply with his speech and landslide victory that he was being considered a possible presidential candidate for 2008. Such predictions frightened Michelle, who worried that the unreasonable expectations could hurt him and their family. She tried to caution people by telling them not to expect too much of Barack. She said, "Maybe one day he will do something to warrant all this attention. The only thing I'm telling people in Illinois is that 'Barack is not our savior.'"[43]

Single Parenting Again

The Obamas decided not to move their family to Washington, D.C., when Barack became a senator. He went there alone. He spent Monday through Thursday in the nation's capital and then flew home to be with his family for the weekend.

Michelle wanted to keep working, and they did not want to disrupt the lives of Malia and Sasha. Michelle was excelling in her own career as Barack embarked on the new part of his. She was promoted to vice president of community and external affairs at the University of Chicago. The promotion came soon after Barack was elected to the Senate, which raised some questions about whether her title and salary were earned. This was deeply frustrating to Michelle, who continued to work hard in her positions. She told the *Chicago Tribune*, "It's just like, dang, is that what you think? Is that who you think we are? What could I do where I would get credit for it completely?"[44]

Proving her point was easy as Michelle launched new programs in her role that benefited the least fortunate of the South Side. The Urban Health Initiative would help bring doctors to neighborhoods that were underserved in health care services. The cost to residents would be minimal, and it would hopefully improve health in the area. Michelle became the face of this program and known to the community and board of trustees alike.

A Big Yes

At the end of 2006, Barack faced an important decision: Should he run for president? When Michelle first heard the idea, she wished he would be conservative about that path and wait a few more years to run so he was fully prepared. In December, when the family went to Hawaii for their traditional Christmas vacation, he and Michelle discussed the subject during their long walks on the beach. Barack has admitted, "Her initial instinct was to say no."[45]

Michelle's hesitation arose from her fears that the campaign would further disrupt her family's life. For the first time, she would have to be a significant part of the campaign, and she realized the effort that was expected of her. She also knew Barack would be subjected to harsh political attacks by his opponents. Michelle worried that Barack would be harmed by those who did not want an African American president. Her fear was not unfounded. Barack did receive death threats, and the Secret Service began protecting their family more than a year before the election, the earliest a presidential candidate had ever received such security.

Michelle knew Barack would not run if she said no, so she considered every scenario, including the dark and scary. She wanted to be emotionally prepared for anything that could

Michelle said she was worried about speaking on the campaign trail for Barack. She did not want to be asked a question she did not know how to answer.

happen during the campaign. Eventually, Michelle realized she had to say yes because she believed that he was a good man who could be a good president. However, she also did not believe he would win or even make it to the general election. Recognizing the concessions she would be making, Michelle had Barack make some in return. She told him he could not neglect their children—during the campaign, he frequently had videocalls with Malia and Sasha—and he had to quit smoking. She also made him promise that if he won the election, he would get his daughters a dog, which they badly wanted.

Barack announced his candidacy on February 10, 2007. As Michelle stood on stage with her family in Springfield, she accepted she had a role to play in the coming months. Yet, she would not mold herself to be only what was expected: "I know the stereotype I was meant to inhabit, the immaculately groomed doll-wife with the painted-on smile … This was not me and never would be. I could be supportive, but I couldn't be a robot."[46] It would be this fire and approachable quality that would make her name on the campaign trail shine just as brightly as her husband's.

On the Road

When Barack announced his candidacy, Michelle agreed to work only part-time even though she enjoyed her job. Michelle devoted herself to campaigning and caring for her daughters, who would see their father in person even less while he was campaigning around the nation. Maintaining stability, Michelle knew, was her job: "What I am not willing to do is hand my kids over to my mom and say, 'We'll see you in two years.' … There has to be a balance and there will be a balance."[47] To make her daughters' lives more normal, Michelle spent as much time as possible with them because Barack was always traveling. To maintain such a schedule, she not only cut her working hours again but kept her campaign trips short, usually being away for just one day.

Barack entered the race 11 months before the first Democratic primary. His biggest rival was New York senator Hillary Clinton, whose husband, Bill, was U.S. president from 1993 to 2001. Barack was the first black candidate and Hillary was the first female candidate in U.S. history to have such a good chance to be elected president. Many Democrats were disappointed that two historic candidates were battling each other for the nomination.

However, Barack had Michelle on his side. Michelle's ability to connect with other women helped Barack compete with Clinton for female voters. She was especially effective in talking to other working mothers. In Austin, Texas, in August 2007, she said,

Fears in the Spotlight

Michelle, though continuously connecting with voters and successfully appearing on TV shows and in interviews, worried that what she said could harm Barack's chances at the presidency. Columnist Maureen Dowd criticized her for speaking about Barack's shortcomings, such as not picking up his socks at home, but it was being reduced to the sound bites of TV news and phrases like "Harvard-educated" that got to Michelle when she had time to think about it: "Quietly I worried that as my visibility as Barack Obama's wife rose, the other parts of me were dissolving from view." She speculated that some might have preferred for her to be the typical political wife with the "painted-on smile and the adoring gaze."[1] Following the Iowa caucuses, Michelle did take leave from her job to keep up the schedule that was expected of her as a political spouse and the mother to two young girls.

1. Michelle Obama, *Becoming*. New York, NY: Crown Publishing Group, 2018, p. 241.

I don't know about you, but as a mother, wife, professional, campaign wife, whatever it is that's on my plate, I'm drowning. And nobody's talking about these issues. In my adult lifetime, I felt duped. People told me, "You can do it all. Just stay the course, get your education and you can raise a child, stay thin, be in shape, love your man, look good and raise healthy children." That was a lie.[48]

She was so effective and popular that Barack began describing her as the "love of my life, the rock of the Obama family [and] the closer on the campaign trail."[49]

Out of Context

At campaign appearances, Michelle told her story of growing up on the South Side of Chicago and her family life. She talked about her dislike of politics and worries about Barack running for office. She liked telling her own story and believed she was finding her voice the more she told it. On February 18, 2008, in Milwaukee, Wisconsin, Michelle made a speech much like those she had made elsewhere. She said, in part, "For the first time in my adult lifetime I am really proud of my country, and not just because Barack has done well, but because I think people are hungry for change."[50] This small part of her about 40-minute speech had been recorded, and Michelle began to be criticized for not loving the United States until it looked like voters might elect her husband president.

It would not be the first time Michelle spoke in a way some people did not like. In discussing the nation's bitter political mood, she repeatedly said the United States had become a mean country. Michelle was just being honest: "My view on this [criticism] is I'm just trying to be myself, trying to be as authentic as I can be. I can't pretend to be somebody else."[51] Though the criticism sometimes stung, she knew she could not respond to it. However, she did take some time to polish her stump speech—a similar speech given over and over by

The night Barack won the Democratic presidential nomination, he and Michelle were seen giving each other a fist bump, which some people said linked them to terrorist groups. It was simply a playful gesture between the couple.

Matters of Race

Michelle's presence in the campaign distinctly helped lend Barack even more credibility with African American voters across the nation. Author Melissa Harris-Perry summed up the effect of Michelle's race on Barack's campaign:

Had he married a white woman, he would have signaled that he had chosen whiteness, a consistent visual reminder that he was not on the African American side. Michelle anchored him. Part of what we as African Americans like about Barack is the visual image of him in the White House, and it would have been stunningly different without Michelle and those brown-skinned girls.[1]

1. Quoted in Peter Slevin, *Michelle Obama: A Life*. New York, NY: Alfred A. Knopf, 2015, p. 214.

someone during a political campaign—and answers to avoid similar misunderstandings in the future.

White House Bound

Michelle crisscrossed the nation for nearly two years. She spoke at the Democratic National Convention and to crowds of a thousand or more in states around the country. Michelle made more solo appearances than any other presidential candidate's spouse ever. She was on the road right up to the November 4 election, when Barack scored a landslide victory over Republican candidate John McCain. It was fitting that she shared the spotlight with Barack on election night during a rousing, emotional celebration at Grant Park in

Chicago, which was only a few miles from the family's Hyde Park home.

The Obamas strode on stage with their children to the thunderous cheers of tens of thousands of people. When Barack and Michelle kissed, the love they had for each other was apparent to the entire world. She remembers the night as being far too much to process: "Here is where I felt like our family got launched out of a cannon and into some strange underwater universe. Things felt slow and aqueous and slightly distorted, even if we were moving quickly."[52]

Chapter Five

Taking On the White House

The First Lady of the United States does not have an official role within the U.S. government. Unlike the president or Supreme Court justices, she has no duties written out in the Constitution. Therefore, it has been up to each First Lady to make the job her own. As Michelle told *Vogue* shortly before leaving the White House,

> I could have spent eight years doing anything, and at some level, it would have been fine. I could have focused on flowers. I could have focused on décor. I could have focused on entertainment. Because any First Lady, rightfully, gets to define her role. There's no legislative authority; you're not elected. And that's a wonderful gift of freedom.[53]

The First Black First Lady

Early on, Michelle recognized the pressure to use her public platform well was doubled because of her race. She felt that she would have to work hard to reach those Americans who might not immediately relate to her because of her skin color: "Not for one second did I think I'd be sliding into some glamorous,

Michelle held the Bible for Barack during his swearing in as president of the United States on January 20, 2009. She has since said she remembers it being freezing cold on stage!

Michelle inherited the job of First Lady from Laura Bush.
Michelle remembers meeting her soon after Barack won
the election and realizing that the Bushes were some of the
very few people who would understand the challenges of a
transition to the White House.

easy role. Nobody who has the words 'first' and 'black' attached to them ever would. I stood at the foot of the mountain knowing I'd need to climb my way into favor."[54]

With this in mind, Michelle spent time assembling her team at the White House, working to understand what was expected of the First Lady and what she wanted to bring to the role—or take away from it. Traditionally, the First Lady plans certain events and parties, a pastime Michelle did not look forward to. However, she realized she could put her own mark on the events instead of following tradition to the letter. For example, instead of simply hosting a luncheon, she incorporated a community service component to the afternoon. She chose art for the White House that included more African American artists, including the first female African American artist to be displayed in the White House. She wrote, "I knew what mattered to me. I didn't want to be some sort of well-dressed ornament who showed up at parties and ribbon cuttings. I wanted to do things that were purposeful and lasting."[55]

Living in the White House

Michelle, Barack, and their daughters moved into the White House residence in January 2009. The residence includes the second and third floors of the iconic building. They also brought Michelle's mother, Marian, to help with Sasha and Malia—though she was reluctant to leave her Chicago home. As is common, the Obamas hired a decorator to make the residence feel more like home, prioritizing the setup of the girls' and Marian's rooms when the transition between the Obamas and Bushes occurred.

However homey the décor might have been, though, Michelle told *Vogue* in late 2016 that living is the White House is "isolating."[56] She has likened living there to staying at a really nice hotel: There are always fresh flowers, it is very clean, and the staff is always trying to make your day better without being underfoot. It is also very quiet, as each window is outfitted with special glass that can stop bombs

Even though they lived in the most famous house in America, the Obamas still found time to spend together doing normal things such as watching TV.

and bullets. The home is always surrounded by members of the Secret Service working to keep those within its walls safe. The First Family is mostly unable to leave the house without an escort, much less undetected. Michelle found this difficult, sometimes just wanting to run to a nearby CVS alone.

Life at the White House had many positives, too. First of all, the residence is quite large, allowing each girl and Marian their own spacious room. Michelle used an interior dressing room space as a personal office—and to wear her most comfortable clothes and just watch TV out of sight. Additionally,

Michelle and Barack were able to make the White House a bit more welcoming. They made sure their daughters could go to the kitchen on their own to find snacks. They offered the staff a more casual uniform some days. Chief among the positives of living at the White House was how often Michelle and the girls saw Barack. Since his office in the West Wing was just downstairs from the residence, he was home for dinner just about every night.

It Starts with the Garden

Before the Obamas moved into the White House, Michelle had one idea of what she might like to do while First Lady: grow the first vegetable garden at the White House since Eleanor Roosevelt was First Lady. She had begun really engaging with healthier eating a few years before when she realized her children's diets were erring more toward the easy than the fresh and healthy. She had begun working with a young chef named Sam Kass, and the family had started incorporating more dishes starring vegetables and eating with the seasons. By planting a garden at the White House, she hoped to bring more awareness to nutrition, particularly for children. Since Barack was working toward a universal health care initiative, Michelle saw her bud of an idea growing into something that could support his political goal.

Michelle and her staff worked for months to have their garden project approved by the National Park Service and agreed to by the White House groundskeepers. Eventually, they were given 1,100 square feet (102 sq m) on the iconic South Lawn. They officially broke ground for the garden on March 20, 2009. A couple weeks later, Michelle, the U.S. secretary of agriculture, and kids from a nearby elementary school started planting broccoli, carrots, peas, herbs, berries, and more. The media was invited to cover the event, but Michelle soon forgot they were there while digging in the dirt and fielding questions from the kids about why the president was not helping. Working with children was a theme she would return to again and again as First Lady: "Kids made

Mom-in-Chief

While campaigning, Michelle said that should their family make it to the White House her number one focus would be taking care of the family. She called herself "mom-in-chief." To those familiar with her accomplishments, this phrase caused them to worry she would not use her position to make a real difference.

What Michelle meant was that she had young children whose well-being simply had to come first:

If we pared back all the pomp and circumstance—the fairy-tale unreality of moving into a big house that came with chefs, a bowling alley, and a swimming pool—what Barack and I were doing was something no parent really wants to do: yanking our kids midyear out of a school they loved, taking them away from their friends, and plopping them into a new house and new school without a whole lot of notice.[1]

She and Barack would be very protective of their daughters throughout his time in office. As they grew up in the spotlight of their father's presidency, they would never do press. They would be photographed, Michelle knew, but she tried to keep their lives as private and normal as possible. This included carefully choosing a

me feel like myself again. To them I wasn't a spectacle. I was just a nice, kinda-tall lady."[57]

The garden was just the first step toward Michelle's bigger platform: a multifaceted plan that would work toward battling childhood obesity. Before announcing it, Michelle and her staff worked for another year talking to people in the food industry about making products better for the health

In April 2009, the family finally brought home the dog the Obama girls wanted. Bo, a Portuguese water dog (shown here), was often called the First Dog. Sunny, another Portuguese water dog, became part of the family in 2013.

school for them before moving to Washington as well as working with the Secret Service to make it possible for the girls to go for ice cream with their friends, play sports, do school activities, and, later, go to the high school prom.

1. Michelle Obama, *Becoming.* New York, NY: Crown Publishing Group, 2018, p. 291.

of children and families. She spoke with the Food and Drug Administration about creating better nutrition labels for foods. Finally, she worked with Barack, and he created the Task Force on Childhood Obesity to support her efforts. The plan launched in February 2010 and was called Let's Move! As Michelle outlined what she and her team had already accomplished, including partnerships with TV networks and professional sports leagues to support a campaign called 60 Minutes of Play a Day, she felt energized: "I was beginning to realize that all the things that felt odd to me about my new existence—the strangeness of fame, the hawkeyed attention paid to my image, the vagueness of my job description—could

The White House Kitchen Garden provided produce for meals at the White House for all of Barack's time in office. Since not all of it could be used at the White House, some produce was donated to a local nonprofit that worked with the homeless.

be marshaled in service of real goals … Here, finally, was a way to show my full self."[58] A year later, Michelle would work hard toward the passage of a nutrition bill in Congress that would help increase access to better-quality food in schools and more.

Using Pop Culture

Over the course of her time as First Lady, Michelle would become a pop culture fixture, familiar to American citizens of all ages. From her appearances on shows from *Sesame Street* to *The Ellen DeGeneres Show*, the public felt like they knew her, that she was fun and relatable—and often seemed removed from politics. However, Michelle did not do all of it for fun. She knew that through these mediums she could reach more people about the topics that mattered to her, including Let's Move! programs, education, female empowerment, and caring for military families. Michelle later wrote, "I was learning how to connect my message to my image, and in this way I could direct the American gaze."[1] Sometimes, this meant she was dancing with Jimmy Fallon or singing in the car with James Corden. She had a push up contest with Ellen DeGeneres—and won. As Michelle told *Variety* in 2016, "What I have never been afraid of is to be a little silly, and you can engage people that way. My view is, first you get them to laugh, then you get them to listen."[2]

1. Michelle Obama, *Becoming*. New York, NY: Crown Publishing Group, 2018, p. 372.

2. Quoted in Ted Johnson, "Michelle Obama Interview: How FLOTUS Used Pop Culture Stardom to Make an Impact," *Variety*, August 23, 2016. variety.com/2016/biz/features/michelle-obama-interview-first-lady-pop-culture-1201842132.

Michelle the Mentor

Early in 2009, Michelle traveled with Barack to England. There, she met the queen of England, Elizabeth II, but it was a visit to a girls' school made up of 90 percent minority groups that shaped some of Michelle's time as First Lady. When speaking to the students at Elizabeth Garrett Anderson School, Michelle saw all that they would have to overcome. She saw herself in them, and she told them they were the ones who could control where their lives would lead. The hope she saw in them inspired her—and she hugged as many as she could before she left. The experience so moved her that she stayed in touch with girls from the school and made many other similar trips as she traveled the world as the First Lady of the United States.

In addition to this visit, Michelle spent time at schools in the Washington, D.C., area. Soon after becoming First Lady, she started a mentoring program at the White House, pairing high school girls from these schools with women working at the White House. Michelle and the other mentors met with these girls about once a month every month Michelle was First Lady. She wanted these girls to gain the same things she hoped for her daughters: "That in learning to feel comfortable at the White House, they'd go on to feel comfortable and confident in any room, sitting at any table, raising their voices inside any group."[59]

Let's Move!, her mentoring program, and her frequent visits to schools and colleges across the country and around the world showed just how important Michelle believed young people to be. She worked hard to bring children to the White House for all kinds of other events, too, including music and arts events. She wanted to open up the world to children who might not otherwise have the opportunity. She told the *Washington Post* in 2010, "The more experiences kids have, the more things that they see, the more things that they know to want. We want to lift young people up. The country needs to be mindful that we have all these diamonds out there, and it would be a shame not to invest in the talents."[60]

Michelle and the girls in the mentoring program sometimes just talked. Other times, they visited the Supreme Court or saw famous dance companies. It was all part of a larger mission to broaden their worldview and build their confidence.

Joining Forces

Even though part of her husband's job would be to serve as commander-and-chief of the armed forces of the United States, Michelle did not know much about the military when she became First Lady. She learned quickly by visiting military hospitals such as Walter Reed National Military Medical Center in Washington, D.C. She spent hours visiting wounded soldiers home from overseas and their families, and listened to their struggles. She met young women who feared for husbands out on dangerous assignments, not knowing what would happen to their small children should they not come home. She found out how difficult it was for some military spouses to find work in their fields as they moved from base to base almost yearly. She wrote, "What I saw of military life left me humbled. As long as I'd been alive, I'd never encountered the kind of fortitude and loyalty that I found in those rooms [of military hospitals]."[61] These and other difficulties led her and Dr. Jill Biden, wife of Vice President Joe Biden, to start Joining Forces in 2011.

The initiative aimed to better support veterans and their families as well as aid servicemen and women and their families while serving on active duty. The Joining Forces team worked with medical professionals around the country to give them better training to deal with veterans' health care. They spoke with state governors about making it easier to transfer credentials and work licenses between states as military spouses moved around with their service member. Joining Forces also aimed to help veterans find jobs and get more education.

With this initiative, Michelle again showed her ability to connect with all kinds of Americans and her determination to not only draw attention to an issue but also make a difference in its future.

Fashion Icon

What the First Lady wears and does with her hair is important. It can set a tone for an event or underline a message she or the president is trying to put across. Michelle learned early on as a political spouse that people looked at what she wore and made decisions about what kind of person she was. Knowing this, she was able to choose her outfits accordingly.

In October 2008, she appeared on *The Tonight Show with Jay Leno*. That week in the news, it had come out that Sarah Palin, the Republican candidate for vice president, had a clothing budget of $150,000. Leno then asked Michelle how much her outfit had cost. When she responded it was from the familiar clothing line J. Crew, found in malls across America, she was letting the public know she was not just another elitist politician's wife. She was one of them.

That did not mean she did not wear Gucci or other couture creations—she did, to much acclaim. As she moved into the role as First Lady, Michelle's fashion choices were scrutinized, idolized, and meticulously documented on fashion blogs, in magazines, and on TV. She was known for wearing bold colors and prints, showing off her toned arms, and wearing cardigans when she was cold—even if they did not particularly match the occasion. Her movement from high fashion designers to everyday choices many Americans themselves could own gave her style an accessibility as well as an aspirational quality.

Some people criticized Michelle for letting fashion conversations occur as often as they did. However, her choices often had a subtle point, and many others came to her defense. For example, she wore gowns with ties to the countries represented at state dinners. In a retrospective of her fashion, the *New York Times* reported,

Mrs. Obama understood that fashion was a means to create an identity for an administration. But unlike any other first lady, instead of seeing it as part of a uniform to which she had to conform, with the attendant rules and strictures that implies, she saw it as a way to frame her own independence and points of difference, add to her portfolio and amplify her husband's agenda.[62]

Michelle's style has been chronicled by fashion bloggers throughout her time as First Lady and even after she left the White House.

Furthermore, the clothes and the hairstyles called even more attention to the First Lady, which was sometimes desirable, according to Michelle: "We take our bangs and we stand in front of important things that the world needs to see. And eventually, people stop looking at the bangs and they start looking at what we're standing in front of."[63]

A Second Term

Even as Michelle's profile got higher, she still spent time with friends, visiting the presidential retreat at Camp David and meeting them for dinner. Valerie Jarrett, who served as an adviser to Barack in the West Wing, told *Vogue* in 2016 that Michelle always stayed grounded in her role as First Lady: "She has this extraordinary ability to meet people where they are. And I think that's hard to do from the lofty perch of the White House. But she has never climbed up on the perch! I've never met anybody with quite that gift before."[64]

Michelle needed this ability as her days as First Lady grew to be full of meetings, events, and connecting with her daughters. As Barack's campaign for reelection began, Michelle knew the pace would only increase. Four years in, Michelle felt invested in continuing the work they had begun in the White House.

Chapter Six

Leaving
a Legacy

On July 25, 2016, Michelle made a speech at the Democratic National Convention. Though she had spoken there in support of Barack's presidential runs in both 2008 and 2012, this speech resonated differently. First of all, Michelle, the first black First Lady, was historically endorsing Hillary Clinton to be the first female president of the United States. She also used the spotlight to confidently address the divisive and often ugly lead-up to the 2016 presidential race as well as her own responses to challenges she and Barack had faced in office. Their motto, she said, when dealing with bullies is: "when they go low, we go high."[65]

Throughout Barack's second presidential campaign and term in office, Michelle had to find ways to execute her vision as First Lady even in the face of criticism of herself and her husband. Barack faced inconsistent approval ratings because of a stubborn Congress's refusal to work with him on many issues, but Michelle's public approval rating soared to almost 80 percent. She met with victims of gun violence and natural disasters. She launched new programs focusing on education. All the while, she was also a mother, watching her daughters continue to grow and become more independent—and beginning to think about what came after life at the White House.

The Second Time Around

Michelle and Barack started working the reelection campaign in the fall of 2011. Michelle worked hard to connect with those she met as well as continue pushing initiatives such as Let's Move! to greater success. She felt that she was coming into her power as First Lady and able to use her platform to bring attention to issues important to her, as well as the importance of voting in the 2012 election.

In September 2012, Michelle spoke at the Democratic National Convention as Barack looked to win the party's nomination for president ahead of the November election. Again, she was a closer for the campaign, bringing those in attendance to their feet at the end of her speech. Her authenticity and conviction shone through as she stated a principle she had been including in her career as far back as Sidley & Austin: "When you've worked hard and done well and walked through that doorway of opportunity, you do not slam it shut behind you. No. You reach back, and you give other folks the same chances that helped you succeed."[66]

Despite this confident proclamation, Michelle was tired after the year of campaigning. So, when the polls closed and Barack's win over Republican Mitt Romney was official, Michelle felt a sense of relief: "When these next four years were over, we'd be truly done, which made me happiest of all. No more campaigning, no more sweating out strategy sessions or polls or debates or approval ratings, ever again. The end of our political life was finally in sight."[67]

Speak Now

Michelle did not feel like she could rest as the second term in the White House dawned. She felt the need to represent

Michelle's speech at the 2012 Democratic National Convention in Charlotte, North Carolina, centered on connecting with the middle class. She also said that she loved Barack even more that day than she had four years before.

the struggles of African Americans, particularly women, who had come before her and to do them proud:

> I put this on myself as pressure, a driving need not to screw anything up. Though I was thought of as a popular First Lady, I couldn't help but feel haunted by the ways I'd been criticized, by the people who'd made assumptions about me based on the color of my skin.[68]

Nonetheless, she found the second term easier because the learning curve was not quite so steep.

Michelle's voice was heard on even more issues in her second term as First Lady as she used both formal speeches and social media to reach the American people. She congratulated those who publicly came out as gay, clearly supporting same-sex marriage. She spoke about gun violence after the shootings at Sandy Hook Elementary School, and the death of a teen girl from Michelle's old Chicago neighborhood saddened and outraged her.

A primary focus became launching programs focused on education. In 2014, the Reach Higher Initiative encouraged young people across the country to continue their education after high school, whether that be through a two- or four-year college or more or through a professional training program. Michelle wanted young people to have more support so they could complete their education. The following year, Michelle worked with Barack and the U.S. government to start Let Girls Learn, a program aiding girls worldwide in finding and finishing their education.

Even after almost eight years in the White House and nearly 20 years as a political spouse, Michelle was not fond of politics. However, when the 2016 election cycle came around, she let her opinions be known: She supported Hillary Clinton for the Democratic nomination and for president. In a speech that called for change and respect among Americans—and subtly pointed out the problems with the opposition—Michelle again impressed people at the Democratic National Convention and

Growing Girls

Michelle wanted to inspire girls around the world to seek their education, but she also had two girls quickly growing into young women to guide right in front of her. She and Barack tried to keep Sasha's and Malia's lives somewhat normal, including having their Secret Service agents wear plainclothes. They found a way to allow Malia's date to drive her to the prom—even though he picked her up at the White House and had a Secret Service escort traveling behind. As the girls got older and their interest waned, Michelle no longer made them attend many events at the White House. She recognized that her daughters were finding their way in the world and she was simply an observer to a lot of it.

Being the mom-in-chief brought some unique challenges, often to do with her visibility when in public and the difficulty of travel. Michelle wrote that she went to New York City to visit colleges with Malia and ended up causing too much commotion being part of the tour of Columbia University. Michelle ended up having to wait out the tour in a room deemed safe by the Secret Service, offering her a few moments of reflection: "I felt a kind of loneliness that probably had less to do with the fact that I was by myself killing time in a windowless room and more to do with the idea that, like it or not, the future was coming, that our first baby was going to grow up and leave."[1] Michelle chose to sit out subsequent college visits, instead sending trusted members of her staff.

1. Michelle Obama, *Becoming*, New York, NY: Crown Publishing Group, 2018, p. 394.

the millions watching at home with her eloquence. It was telling that someone so long exposed to the ugliness of politics would agree to speak when it was no longer required of her.

ity College
w York

Every year, Michelle gives a few commencement speeches at colleges and high schools around the country. She has tried to pick places that would have a harder time bringing in a well-known speaker.

In fact, Michelle had a code for herself on this very topic: "When it came to speaking publicly about anything or anyone in the political sphere: I said only what I absolutely believed and what I absolutely felt."[69]

Beyond the White House

As the Obamas prepared to turn the White House over to President Donald Trump, who had defeated Hillary Clinton, Michelle tried to leave her stamp. She had an official china setting made. She ensured that the White House Kitchen Garden she cared for so much would remain part of the South Lawn. She had it expanded and entrusted it to the National Park Service before leaving office.

At just 53 years old the day she left the White House, Michelle knew being First Lady was not the end of her work in public life. She told *Vogue* that, as she left the White House, she would continue to dedicate her time to public service, but what exactly she would do, she had not yet planned out. The main focus of her speech at the 2016 Democratic National Convention foreshadowed that her focus going forward would have a lot to do with bettering the lives of children:

> *This election and every election is about who will have the power to shape our children for the next four or eight years of their lives ... I want a leader who is ... worthy of*

The Obama family left the White House on January 20, 2017.

The Obama Foundation

The Obama Foundation was founded in 2014. One of its first tasks was to oversee the building of the Obama Presidential Center in Jackson Park on Chicago's South Side. It is also the main way Michelle and Barack have continued their public service work in the Chicago community, in the national community, and around the world. The Obama Foundation has programs working to train and improve community leaders, support young men of color through mentorship, and invite young people to training events geared toward civic leadership skills.

One of the major initiatives Michelle is involved with as part of the Obama Foundation is the Global Girls Alliance. It works to support more and better education for girls around the world by providing resources and connections for global organizations to use, raising money, and spreading the word about the importance of education among girls.

In 2017, the Obama Foundation hosted its first summit. It featured artists, politicians, and community leaders looking to find solutions to many different kinds of problems.

my girls' promise and all our kids' promise, a leader who will be guided every day by the love and hope and impossibly big dreams that we all have for our children.[70]

Her final words as First Lady echoed this path as well: "I want our young people to know that they matter, that they belong … Empower yourself with a good education. Then get out there and use that education to build a country worthy of your boundless promise."[71]

Still, for much of the rest of 2017, both Michelle and Barack stayed fairly quiet. They chose to continue living in Washington until Sasha finished high school in 2019. They both gave speeches, traveled, and were hard at work writing books for a joint deal reportedly worth about $30 million. They also signed a deal to produce content for Netflix.

Michelle's book, *Becoming,* was published on November 13, 2018. Other First Ladies had written books following their time in the White House, including

There is no question that Michelle Obama has had an impact on the American people and the office of First Lady.

Laura Bush and Hillary Clinton, but Michelle's promotion of her book was structured a little differently than the book tours of past First Ladies. Instead of simply visiting bookstores to read an excerpt and sign some books for readers, Michelle appeared in arenas around the country. The first stop was the United Center in Chicago, an event that sold out with 14,000 in attendance. The event included a conversation between Michelle and Oprah Winfrey about the content of the book, which covers Michelle's life from birth through the end of her time as First Lady, including reflections on all that she has gone through in her life. By the end of November, *Becoming* had become the best-selling book of 2018, selling more than 1.1 million copies in just a few weeks.

Book sales are simply one indication of the impression Michelle made on the American people over eight years as First Lady. Many have said since she left the White House how much Michelle as the First Lady meant to them and to the country. Actress Rashida Jones reflected on all the roles Michelle played while at the White House in an article for *The New York Times Magazine*. She was a mother, dog-owner, campaigner, pop culture icon, fashionista, and incredible speaker. Jones wrote, "Michelle Obama will have her own legacy, separate from her husband's. And it will be that she was the first first lady to show women that they don't have to choose. That it's okay to be everything."[72] Feminist leader Gloria Steinem echoed Jones's praise: "Michelle Obama may have changed history in that most powerful way—by example."[73]

To Michelle, with her dedication to young people, it might be the words of girls that let her know her legacy is important and secure. In 2016, PBS asked girls what Michelle Obama meant to them. A 17-year-old girl from Tennessee named Inara Abernathy said, "She's strong and beautiful and makes me feel beautiful, too. I feel like I can accomplish things when I think about her."[74] Kassidy Carey, a Virginia high school student, expressed that Michelle made it clear that girls weren't only girls: "She makes us feel like people who actually have opinions that matter and who can fight for what we believe in."[75]

Michelle has made clear that despite all that she has been able to accomplish and all the lives she has inspired, she has no desire to run for office—especially not president. She does, however, have every intention of forging ahead as an example to all girls and boys of any color or background that they can find their places at any table—or in any portrait gallery—they want.

Notes

Introduction: A Groundbreaking Role Model

1. Jessica Curry, "Looking Up to Michelle Obama," *New York Times*, March 12, 2018. www.nytimes.com/2018/03/12/opinion/michelle-obama-portrait-sherald-parker.html?rref=collection%2Ftimestopic%2FObama%2C%20Michelle.

2. Curry, "Looking Up to Michelle Obama."

3. Curry, "Looking Up to Michelle Obama."

4. Curry, "Looking Up to Michelle Obama."

5. Quoted in David Mack, "Michelle Obama Met (And Danced With) the Little Girl Who Was Mesmerized by Her Portrait," BuzzFeed News, March 6, 2018. www.buzzfeednews.com/article/davidmack/michelle-obama-little-girl-portrait-parker-curry-meet-dance.

6. Quoted in Kevin Liptak and Bonney Kapp, "Michelle Obama in Final Speech: 'I hope I've made you proud,'" CNN, January 13, 2017. www.cnn.com/2017/01/06/politics/michelle-obama-final-speech/index.html.

Chapter One: From the South Side to the Ivy League

7. Quoted in David Colbert, *Michelle Obama: An American Story*. New York, NY: Houghton Mifflin Harcourt, 2009, p. 17.

8. Michelle Obama, "Michelle Obama's Remarks at the Democratic Convention," *New York Times*, August 25, 2008. elections.nytimes.com/2008/president/conventions/videos/transcripts/20080825_obama_speech.html.

9. Quoted in Colbert, *Michelle Obama*, p. 17.

10. Michelle Obama, *Becoming*. New York, NY: Crown Publishing Group, 2018, p. 25.

11. Obama, *Becoming*, p. 22.

12. Quoted in Rebecca Johnson, "The Natural," *Vogue*, September 2007. www.vogue.com/article/michelle-obama-the-natural.

13. Quoted in Maria L. La Ganga, "It's All About Priorities for Michelle Obama," *Los Angeles Times*, August 22, 2007. articles.latimes.com/2007/aug/22/nation/na-michelle22.

14. Obama, *Becoming*, p. 66.

15. Obama, *Becoming*, p. 72.

16. Obama, *Becoming*, p. 80.

17. Obama, *Becoming*, p. 89.

Chapter Two: Harvard, Law, and Love

18. Quoted in Sally Jacobs, "Learning to Be Michelle Obama," *Boston Globe*, June 15, 2008. archive.boston.com/news/nation/articles/2008/06/15/learning_to_be_michelle_obama/?page=1.

19. Michelle LaVaughn Robinson, "Princeton-Educated Blacks and the Black Community," senior thesis, Princeton University, 1985.

20. Quoted in Peter Slevin, *Michelle Obama: A Life*. New York, NY: Alfred A. Knopf, 2015, p. 115.

21. Quoted in David Mendell, *Obama: From Promise to Power*. New York, NY: Amistad, 2007, pp. 93–94.

22. Obama, *Becoming*, p. 106.

23. Barack Obama, *The Audacity of Hope: Thoughts on Reclaiming the American Dream*. New York, NY: Crown Publishing Group, 2006, p. 330.

24. Obama, *Becoming*, p. 123.

25. Obama, *Becoming*, p. 105.

26. Quoted in Peter Slevin, "Her Heart's in the Race; Michelle Obama on the Campaign Trail and Her Life's Path," *Washington*

Post, November 28, 2007. www.washingtonpost.com/wp-dyn/content/article/2007/11/27/AR2007112702670.html.

27. Obama, *Becoming*, p. 118.

Chapter Three: Big Changes

28. Quoted in Andy Katz, "Brown Coach Robinson Coaching Brother-in-Law Obama, Too," ESPN, September 13, 2007. sports.espn.go.com/ncb/columns/story?columnist=katz_andy&id=3009012.

29. Obama, *Becoming*, p. 132.

30. Obama, *Becoming*, p. 153.

31. Quoted in Richard Wolffe, "Barack's Rock," *Newsweek*, February 25, 2008, p. 29.

32. Quoted in Slevin, *Michelle Obama: A Life*, p. 161.

33. Quoted in Mendell, *Obama: From Promise to Power*, p. 99.

Chapter Four: More Than a Wife and Mother

34. Obama, *Becoming*, p. 173.

35. Obama, *Becoming*, p. 193.

36. Quoted in Slevin, *Michelle Obama: A Life*, p. 173.

37. Quoted in Johnson, "The Natural."

38. Obama, *Becoming*, p. 207.

39. Obama, *Becoming*, p. 205.

40. Quoted in Slevin, "Her Heart's in the Race."

41. Quoted in Rosalind Rossi, "The Woman Behind Obama," *Chicago Sun Times*, January 20, 2007. www.suntimes.com/news/metro/221458,cst-nws-mich21.article.

42. Obama, *Becoming*, p. 216.

43. Quoted in Liza Mundy, *Michelle: A Biography*. New York, NY: Simon & Schuster, 2009, p. 9.

44. Quoted in Slevin, *Michelle Obama: A Life*, p. 193.

45. Quoted in Evan Thomas, "How He Did It," *Newsweek*, January 21, 2008, p. 40.

46. Obama, *Becoming*, p. 231.

47. Quoted in Slevin, *Michelle Obama: A Life*, p. 208.

48. Quoted in La Ganga, "It's All About Priorities for Michelle Obama."

49. Quoted in Sarah Baxter, "America Hails the Rise of a New JFK," *Sunday Times* (London), January 6, 2008.

50. Quoted in Lauren Collins, "The Other Obama: Michelle Obama and the Politics of Candor," *New Yorker*, March 10, 2008. www.newyorker.com/magazine/2008/03/10/the-other-obama.

51. Quoted in Anne E. Kornblut, "Michelle Obama's Career Timeout; For Now, Weight Shifts in Work-Family Tug of War," *Washington Post*, May 11, 2007.

52. Obama, *Becoming*, p. 278.

Chapter Five: Taking On the White House

53. Quoted in Jonathan Van Meter, "Michelle Obama: A Candid Conversation With America's Champion and Mother in Chief," *Vogue*, November 11, 2016. www.vogue.com/article/michelle-obama-december-cover-interview-first-lady-white-house-departure.

54. Obama, *Becoming*, p. 284.

55. Obama, *Becoming*, p. 310.

56. Quoted in Van Meter, "Michelle Obama: A Candid Conversation With America's Champion and Mother in Chief."

57. Obama, *Becoming*, p. 322.

58. Obama, *Becoming*, p. 339.

59. Obama, *Becoming*, p. 357.

60. Quoted in Slevin, *Michelle Obama: A Life*, p. 279.

61. Obama, *Becoming*, p. 345.

62. Vanessa Friedman, "What Michelle Obama Wore and Why It Mattered," *New York Times*, January 14, 2017. www.nytimes.com/2017/01/14/fashion/michelle-obama-first-lady-fashion.html?rref=collection%2Ftimestopic%2FObama%2C%20Michelle.

63. Quoted in Slevin, *Michelle Obama: A Life*, p. 4.

64. Quoted in Van Meter, "Michelle Obama: A Candid Conversation With America's Champion and Mother in Chief."

Chapter Six: Leaving a Legacy

65. "Transcript: Read Michelle Obama's Full Speech from the 2016 DNC," *Washington Post*, July 26, 2016. www.washingtonpost.com/news/post-politics/wp/2016/07/26/transcript-read-michelle-obamas-full-speech-from-the-2016-dnc/?utm_term=.b48693efb1d5.

66. Quoted in Slevin, *Michelle Obama: A Life*, p. 320.

67. Obama, *Becoming*, p. 376.

68. Obama, *Becoming*, p. 366.

69. Obama, *Becoming*, p. 407.

70. "Transcript: Read Michelle Obama's Full Speech from the 2016 DNC," *Washington Post*.

71. Quoted in Liptak and Kapp, "Michelle Obama in Final Speech: 'I hope I've made you proud.'"

72. Rashida Jones, "To the First Lady, With Love," *New York Times Magazine*, October 17, 2016. www.nytimes.com/2016/10/17/t-magazine/michelle-obama-chimamanda-ngozi-adichie-gloria-steinem-letter.html.

73. Gloria Steinem, "To the First Lady, With Love," *New York Times Magazine*, October 17, 2016. www.nytimes.com/2016/10/17/t-magazine/michelle-obama-chimamanda-ngozi-adichie-gloria-steinem-letter.html.

74. Quoted in Leanne Italie, "Michelle Obama's Legacy Spans from Healthy Food to Girls' Empowerment," PBS, December 24, 2016. www.pbs.org/newshour/politics/michelle-obama-legacy.

75. Quoted in Italie, "Michelle Obama's Legacy Spans from Healthy Food to Girls' Empowerment."

Michelle Obama Year by Year

1964

Michelle Robinson is born in Chicago, Illinois, on January 17.

1977

Michelle begins high school at Whitney M. Young.

1981

Michelle graduates from Whitney M. Young and begins school at Princeton University.

1985

Michelle earns her undergraduate degree from Princeton University. She starts attending Harvard Law School.

1988

Michelle graduates from Harvard Law School. She begins working for the law firm Sidley & Austin in Chicago.

1989

Michelle meets and begins dating Barack Obama.

1990

Michelle is present when her close friend, Suzanne Alele, dies.

1991

Michelle's father, Fraser, dies, and she begins working for the mayor of Chicago.

1992

Michelle marries Barack Obama on October 3.

1993

Michelle becomes the executive director of Public Allies Chicago.

1996

Michelle begins working for the University of Chicago.

1997

Barack is sworn in as an Illinois state senator for the first time.

1998

Malia Ann Obama is born on July 4.

2000

Barack runs unsuccessfully for U.S. Congress.

2001

Natasha Marian Obama is born on June 10.

2002

Michelle starts work as executive director for community affairs at University of Chicago Hospitals.

2004

Michelle attends the Democratic National Convention to see Barack speak, and Barack wins a seat in the U.S. Senate.

2005

Michelle attends Barack's swearing in as a U.S. senator in Washington, D.C.

2007

Michelle stands with Barack as he announces his candidacy for president.

2008

Michelle speaks in support of Barack at the Democratic National Convention in Denver, Colorado, on August 25, and on November 4, Michelle officially becomes the incumbent First Lady of the United States as Barack wins the presidency.

2009

Michelle holds the Bible for Barack as he is sworn in as the 44th U.S. president; the Obama family moves to Washington, D.C.; and Michelle attends the groundbreaking of the White House Kitchen Garden.

2010

Michelle launches the Let's Move! campaign.

2011

Michelle and Dr. Jill Biden launch Joining Forces.

2012

Michelle again speaks in favor of her husband at the Democratic National Convention. Barack wins the party's nomination.

2013

Michelle again holds the Bible for Barack as he is sworn in as president for the second time.

2014

The Obama Foundation is established, and Michelle launches the Reach Higher initiative.

2015

Barack and Michelle start Let Girls Learn.

2016

Michelle speaks at the Democratic National Convention in support of Hillary Clinton.

2017

Michelle gives her last speech as First Lady.

2018

The portraits of Michelle and Barack Obama are unveiled in the Smithsonian's National Portrait Gallery, and Michelle's memoir, *Becoming*, is released.

For More Information

Books

Chambers, Veronica. *The Meaning of Michelle: 16 Writers on the Iconic First Lady and How Her Journey Inspires Our Own.* New York, NY: St. Martin's Press, 2018.
In this book, 16 different writers offer their reflections on the importance of Michelle Obama's time as First Lady.

Hodges, Kate. *I Know a Woman: The Inspiring Connections Between the Women Who Have Shaped Our World.* London, UK: Aurum Press, 2018.
Hodges writes about the stories of many inspirational women throughout history and how they influenced each other.

Obama, Barack. *Dreams from My Father: A Story of Race and Inheritance.* New York, NY: Crown Publishing Group, 2007.
Readers interested in learning more about Barack Obama can learn about his past in his first book.

Obama, Michelle. *American Grown: The Story of the White House Kitchen Garden and Gardens Across America.* New York, NY: Crown Publishing Group, 2012.
Readers get an inside look at Michelle Obama's White House Kitchen Garden and learn about the gardens and gardeners that inspired her work.

Obama, Michelle. *Becoming.* New York, NY: Crown Publishing Group, 2018.
Michelle Obama's memoir offers her personal reflections on her childhood, her career, her marriage, and her time in the White House and beyond.

Pastan, Amy. *First Ladies.* New York, NY: DK Publishing, 2017.
This book gives readers a detailed look at First Ladies throughout U.S. history.

Websites

First Ladies of the United States
(www.firstladies.org/biographies/)
Read more about the lives of the First Ladies of the United States at the website for the National First Ladies Library.

Let's Move!
(letsmove.obamawhitehouse.archives.gov/)
Check out more about Michelle's Let's Move! initiative on the White House website.

Michelle Obama on Instagram
(www.instagram.com/michelleobama/?hl=en)
Follow the former First Lady as she continues to make an impact on the world.

Michelle Obama—The White House
(www.whitehouse.gov/about-the-white-house/first-ladies/michelle-obama/)
Michelle Obama's official biography as a former First Lady can be found on the White House website.

The Obama Foundation
(www.obama.org/)
Find out the latest news about Michelle and Barack as well as projects they are involved with.

Index

Picture Credits

About the Author

Kristen Rajczak Nelson has written and edited hundreds of nonfiction books for children on a variety of subjects, from the importance of voting to biographies of inspiring men and women, including the recent Lucent Press title *Lin-Manuel Miranda: From Broadway to the Big Screen*. She received a B.A. in English with a minor in journalism from Gannon University and an M.A. in arts journalism from the S.I. Newhouse School of Public Communications at Syracuse University. She spends her time traveling, trying out new recipes, and exploring the area around her Western New York home with her family.